A Workbook for Crafting, Painting or Stitching

by Sandy Redburn & Shelly Ehbrecht

Crafty Secrets Publications
15430 78A Ave.
Surrey, B.C. Canada
V3S 8R4

ISBN 0-9699410-6-4

Table of Contents

Categories & Themes

There is a smorgasbord of creative supplies and helpful aids for lettering expressions onto an almost endless array of surfaces. Check with your local retail stores for products from the manufacturers listed below.

Permanent Markers
EK Success
(Zig Markers)
611 Industrial Rd.
Carlstadt, NJ 07072-6507
Phone (201) 939-5404
Fax (201) 939-4511

Permanent Markers
Sakura of America
(Pigma® Ink Products)
30780 San Clemente St.
Hayward, CA 94544-7131
Phone (510) 475-8880
Fax (510) 475-0973

Needle Craft Alphabets
ASN Publishing
1455 Linda Vista Drive
San Marcos, CA 92069
Phone (760) 471-2320
Fax (760) 591-0230

Walnut Hollow Farm Inc.
1409 State Road 23
Dodgeville, WI
53533-2112
Phone (608) 935-2341
Fax (608) 935-3029

Introduction

We did it again! We're back with another helping of new Heartwarmin' Expressions! We've had so much fun with our first two books and such a great response that we couldn't resist warming some hearts again.

As many of us look for more simple pleasures in our complex, often stressful world, we have begun to focus more on our family, spirituality, values, friendships, homes and health. By adding some heartwarmin' and humorous expressions to giftware, greetings wearables, seasonal and home decor projects you can create more warm fuzzies and smiles in your life and the lives of those around you.

This third book, "Another 425 Heartwarmin' Expressions" includes past favorite themes, along with two new categories. Be sure to check our fun "Photo Quips" as well as "Proverbs" from all corners of the world. We hope our new third collection will leave your imagination and creative spirit brimming with inspiring ideas.

Thanks Are Due

We would once again like to thank the many creative souls who passed on more of their favorite expressions to be included in this third Heartwarmin' book. A special thanks must go to Brenda Rintisch, Lynn Ujvary and Julie Weibe for their great contributions and creative inspirations.

Please feel free to send us some of your own expressions too. A big thank you to those who do!

We especially need to thank our husbands and daughters for their constant support and creative ideas. After a summer of driving ourselves and them crazy (being a little crazy helps) and wearing out our rhyming dictionary, they were still supportive. They deserve a big round of applause.

A special Heartwarmin' thanks must also go to you, our readers, for your support and response to these books. Have fun spreading smiles!

Sandy & Shelly

Sandy's dedication to inspiring others' creativity includes teaching seminars, writing and publishing books since 1993, including "Crafty Marketing - Jumpstart Your Creative Business". She runs her successful homebased business with the help of her other passion, her husband and three daughters.

Shelly has received her CPD, (Certified Professional Demonstrator Diploma) and enjoys teaching folk art painting and creative lettering classes. She is also a registered nurse on a maternity ward and lives a happy, busy life with her husband and two daughters.

Easy Lettering Tips & Tricks

Lettering is not as hard as you may think and, as you will see throughout this book, by no means does it have to be perfect or for that matter straight! You can do your lettering by free hand, or you can trace our expressions and designs right onto your project.

If you would like your lettering larger, you can recreate any expression using the enlarged alphabets in the back of this book. You may also photocopy any expressions and have them enlarged or reduced to fit your personal needs.

It' s Easy!

1. Use a pencil & ruler. Lettering does not have to be even - just consistent.
2. Hold pens in an upright position.
3. When possible pull your pen rather than push.
4. Add extra embellishments to create different styles.
5. Get bravely creative - but remember practice and patience.

Dot lettering seems to be the most popular and easiest style of printing to reproduce. Remember you do not have to embellish your letters with dots. As you will see, you can change your printing style by adding hearts, stars, flowers, snowflakes, holly, stitching lines and more!

There are countless design books available, with wonderful patterns to which you can trace and add expressions. Look around you for inspiration and designs that you can match with expressions. Once you start, you will find life offers endless "perfect spots" to add a Heartwarmin' Expression or tickle some funny bones.

Trace or pencil on your lettering first, to get your spacing right. A good eraser and see-through plastic ruler are two very helpful tools for lettering.

stressed needle Love twinkle

worms School moo Fun sister grass

Christmas

Macho Kisses

Using Pens & Markers

Using Pens and markers is easy and fun because they are now available in a multitude of tip styles, sizes and colors in both water based and permanent inks. Water based pens work well for a variety of paper crafts, but permanent pigma ink markers won't fade and can be used on a large variety of surfaces. The manufacturers of these markers all agree you should hold your pens in an upright position so the tip has full contact with the writing surface. It may feel a bit awkward but will give you the true essence of the pen tip. You will also find you have better control of your pen when you pull it towards you rather than pushing it away.

Our samples below show how different combinations of pen tips can give your lettering loads of personality and style.

Letters - Pigma Micron 05
Embellishments - Pigma Micron 01

Have a Bloomin Good Day

Letters - Pigma Micron 03

Don't get yer knickers in a knot!

Letters - Zig 08 Millennium
Embellishments - Pigma Micron 01

An old fisherman and the catch of his life live here.

Letters - Zig 08 Millennium, Shade - Pigma Micron 03

DISCOVER WILDLIFE - Have Kids

Letters - Pigma Micron 01

There's snowman I'd rather be with.

Letters - Pigma Micron 03, Embellishments - Zig 01 Millennium

Miracles grow where you plant them.

Sakura Dual-point Identi Pen: Letters - the fine point Embellishments - the extra fine point

Creative Possibilities

Transferring expressions and designs is not difficult. You can mix and match expressions with any pattern and design. Once you decide on an expression and image you want to use, lay tracing paper over it and draw it out. Lay your traced design on your project surface and slip some transfer paper in between your design and prepared surface. Trace the outline with a stylus or empty pen tip. Saral® manufactures a Wax-Free Transfer paper that works on paper, wood, fabric, metal, glass, tile, ceramic, etc. Wax free paper will not clog the tips of your markers and pens. Heat activated transfer pencils also work well on fabric.

Expressions On Wood

There are so many different painting styles, techniques and decorative finishes used on wood today, it can make your head swim. Some popular applications include primitive to fancy overlay stencils, block printing, antiquing, faux finishing, traditional tole painting, pen and ink watercolors, rustic country or folk art painting. You just need to match your design to the right expression and style of lettering.

If you don't have a steady hand for doing your lettering with a paintbrush don't worry, you can cheat and use permanent markers. When you apply dots to letters on wood, use paint rather than your pen tip. Not only will you save the life of your pens, you can create dots faster and more consistent in size using paint. Dots can be made using a brush tip, stylus or embossing tool. We use corsage pins and various plastic headed pins for different size dots. Stick the pins into the eraser tip of a pencil and just dip the head into paint. When using permanent markers for lettering, test any varnish first. Krylon manufactures sprays and varnishes that won't make the ink in permanent markers bleed.

Walnut Hollow manufactures wood burning pens, which are perfect for adding letters and designs you have traced onto wood. We also love using their oil colored pencils on wood projects, available in 36 rich, vibrant and metallic colors.

Expressions On Paper Crafts

Use expressions to create your own special occasion and seasonal decorations, birthday cards, photo memory albums and scrapbooks, framed calligraphy, greeting cards, gift tags, invitations, stationary and wrapping paper. Jazz up your projects with colored pencils and inks, watercolors, metallic markers, glitter pens, decorative punches and scissors, templates, stencils, stickers, rubber stamps, 3D or traditional decoupage, paper mold reliefs and more!

Painting Expressions On Fabric

First pre-wash fabric to remove any sizing and don't use any fabric softener. You can use a heat activated transfer pencil, or place some fabric transfer paper between your design and fabric (following all manufacturers' directions). Before painting your transferred design, place a piece of cardboard under your fabric surface (a cookie sheet will also work). Use fabric paints or regular acrylics mixed with a textile medium. Look for quality brushes recommended for textile painting, fabric markers, or use the mini tips on paint bottles to do your lettering.

Expressions On Glass & Ceramics

Paint expressions on an assortment of dishware, tiles, glasses, vases and decor. You can use traditional ceramic techniques and glazes, or cheat and use the new glass and ceramic paints. DecoArt makes Ultra Gloss, a paint which becomes permanent when baked in your oven. Delta Perm Enamel is a new air drying permanent paint made for glossy and hard to adhere surfaces.

Expressions By Needle & Thread

Stitching includes an array of techniques for applying expressions, using fancy threads, floss, yarns, ribbons or beads. Machine or hand embroidery, hand stitching on felt, needlepoint, cross stitch, plastic canvas, quilted appliqués and silk ribbon embroidery are all popular decorative embellishments. You can stitch expressions on baby bibs to bumper pads, decorative pillows, wall samplers, aprons, linens, sweatshirts, vests, jumpers, jean jackets, boxer shorts, ties, bathrobes and more!

The American School of Needlework (ASN Publishing) is a great source for corss stitch design books including one called *The Ultimate Cross stitch Alphabet Book.* If you don't want to stitch by hand, check out the amazing things you can create with an embroidery machine today!

Embellishing Your Expressions

Depending on the materials and style of your project you can also embellish expressions with raffia, jute, wire, paper twist, ribbons, lace, trims, buttons, charms, shells, fabric motifs, lace appliqués or miniature accessories. To add unique appeal to cloth dolls and animals use short expressions on mini signs or cut out shapes.

You are only limited by your imagination, so go on . . . get creative!

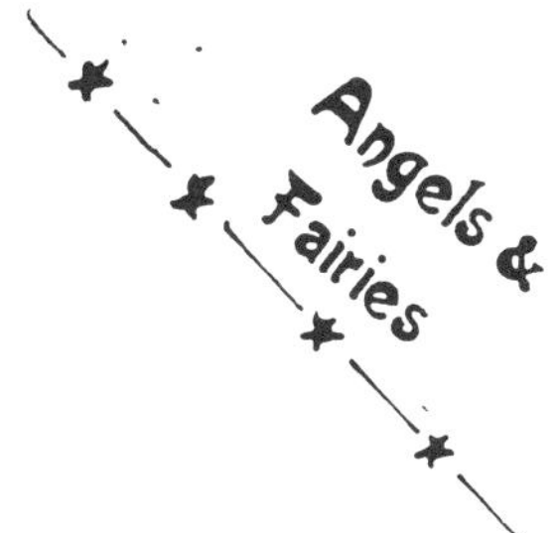

My guardian angel watches over me
and keeps me safe, as safe as can be

Good Night Sweet Prince (Princess)
and flights of angels sing thee to thy rest.

- Shakespeare
Hamlet, V, 2

Wish I may, wish I might
see a wee pixie tonight

Secret Garden
Fairies Gather Here

When the first baby laughed, for the first time,
his laugh broke into a million pieces,
and they all went skipping about.
that was the beginning of fairies

- J.M. Barrie

Angels help radiate his love from above.

Fairy Duties
* Collect lost teeth
* Kiss boo-boos
* sprinkle sleepy dust
* chase away bad dreams

When angels sing....
flowers bloom

If we all acted more angelic
the world would feel more heavenly

Angels are messengers from above,
sent to spread God's light and love.

A wing and a prayer
can take you anywhere.

Guardian angels
from up above
please watch over
those we love

Angels bring comfort from up above,
on wings of faith and whispers of love

Have a fairy enchanting time.

A fairy nice person
&
an old troll
live here.

Sweet enough
to be an angel

God watches over us
with tender loving care
and when we need a helping hand
an angel's always there.

Be an angel,
God loves a helping hand

Don't wait till you get to heaven
to act like an angel.

Blessings

May the road rise up to meet you
May the wind be at your back.

- Irish Blessing

Look after everything
in this world
as if it belongs to God,
it does.

CHOOSE JOY!

Faith shines brightest in the dark.

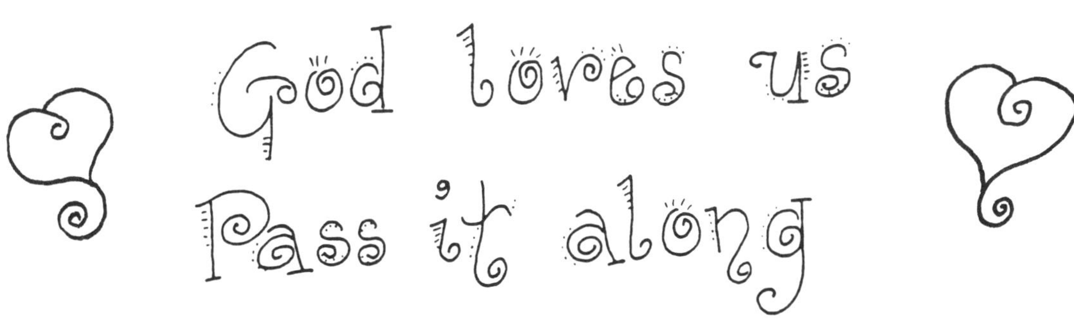

Lord Let Your Love and Grace
Shine Upon and Bless this Place.

He didn't call them the 10 suggestions.

*Better to have riches in your soul,
than in your wallet.*

Life!

Each day is a gift to unfold
Savour each because our present has no mold.

God works in moments.
- French proverb

For today and its blessings,
I owe the world an attitude of gratitude.
- Clarence E. Hodges

There is a special blessing
in my life
YOU

May all the World be richly blessed
With lasting peace and happiness.

Enjoy yourself
these are the good ol' days
you're going to miss one day

God's love is strong.
- Psalm 117:2

Count your blessings
not your cash.

May you live as long as you want
and never want as long as you live

Were there no God,
we would all be in this glorious world
with grateful hearts and no one to thank
- Christine Rossetti

Count your blessings every day
see them grow in every way

There's snowman I'd rather be with

Yo Snow

Cold nose... Warm heart.

Shaped from warm hands and young ♡s

Be warm Inside & Out

There is snow-girl like my girl Frosty

Chill out! I'm a really cool guy just a little bit flakey

WANTED: Summer house to rent (prefer Arctic location or your freezer)

To my Family: Yule always be the best part of Christmas xox

Deck the malls ...... with all my money.

The Christmas present most often returned LOVE

May the spirit of Christmas fill you with love and peace, spreading goodwill that will never cease.

CHRISTMAS

Christmas Blessings
wrapped in warm wishes
tied with joy &
sent with love.

Wise men still adore him.

Wishing you JOY
be-Claus it's Christmas.

Peace on Earth
& Goodwill to All

Wishing you a Christmas brimming
with love, laughter and joyful memories.

Season's Tweetings

The Perfect Man
He's quiet and sweet
and if he gives you any grief
you can bite his head off.

Howdy Ya'll Do?

You're the apple of my eye,
You're the cream of the crop,
You're the ice cream on my pie
and the cherry on top!

Please tell my mom:
Cowboys don't take baths,
we just dust off.

Don't look back,
the posse's gaining

Speak your mind....
But ride a fast horse.

Happiness is:
being a true cowgirl.

Don't get yer knickers in a knot!

Don't Gossip on the Farm Cuz:
the corn have ears,
the potatoes have eyes,
the grass whispers,
and the horses carry tales.

Doggone Good to T-bone

Our dog may be no perfect pedigree
just the perfect mixture we agree!
A mutt.

My dog
is
my
best friend

Just say No to chicken nuggets

NO!

We're only staying together
for the sake of the dog.

My dog doesn't care
if I'm rich, witty or slim,
I'll always be a best friend
to him.

Tweet Dreams

To or not to

I'm not rude.
I've got cat-i-tude!

In this house,
the cat is in charge

Pussed off!

Every life should
have 9 cats!

Home is Where
the meow is

My kitty
makes everyday
purr-fect

Purr-ority
Post
Fur-class
Just for Mew

Cats understand the importance of naps.

How wonderful to do nothing and rest afterwards.

Feline purr-fect tuna-night

When it's raining cats and dogs,
Don't step in the poodles.

I miss ewe
moo and moo
each day.

Bless Ewe

Ewe wooly warm
my ♥

Virgin Wool:
from sheep that run real fast.

We had an udderly mooo-velous time!

There will never be
an udder
quite like you.

Have you ....
herd the moos?

Ewe moo-ve me

The cow:
nature's lawn moo-er.

Toadly Hoppy

Have I toad you lately
how hoppy you make me?

Plan ahead for those rainy days.
Noah did.

FAMILY

Dad,
no matter
how tall I grow
I will always
look up to you

Oh daughter (son) so dear,
We love you more than
all the sand on the beach,
stars in the sky and
clothes on your floor!

DISCOVER WILDLIFE - Have Kids

Babies are such a nice way
to start people. - Herold

Babies are bits
of stardust
blown from the
hand of God
- Larry Barretto

Wildlife Refugee Habitat
(welcome to our games room)

In the whole wide world,
there is nothing more precious
than a baby.

Babies smile when kissed by an angel

We have a minority rule here,
It's called a baby.

Sisterhood is Powerful.

I can't imagine a better brother than you.

Here's a hug and a kiss
for the brother (sister, etc.) I miss.

My sister,
My friend.

It's hard to be humble
when you're a Grandmother.

FAMILY

My Mom is:

♥ my Guardian Angel.
♥ my Heart Mender.
♥ my Best Friend.

Grandmas give out the best
hugs 'n' cookies.

Great Dads
get promoted
to Grand-dads.

You put the GRAND
in Grandmother.

Family is another name for love.

God couldn't be everywhere
that's why he created Godparents.

Mother is the name of God
in the lips and hearts of little children.

- William Thackery

I may not be rich
but I have some priceless jewels.....
my grandchildren.

Best Gramps
I ever saw.

CAUTION:
Grandparents at Play

To a fisherman the sounds of the river
are as musical as any symphony
and twice as compelling. - A.J. McClane

Save the worms
Eat chicken

My wish:
To catch a FAT fish.

If today were a fish,
I'd throw it back.

A fisherman's favourite line....
has a worm on the end of it.

You catch....
You clean.

Haven't had much luck fishing -
but I did marry the catch of my life

Sounds a bit fishy!

Grandpa says....
I'm a keeper.

Gone fishin'
Be back someday

Fishing

The great fishing never stops,
the fish just bite in other spots
TELL ME WHERE!

My Goal:
Fish more,
Work less.

Fishing
it's the reel thing

FISHING

The art of casting, trolling, jigging
or spinning,
while freezing, sweating, swatting
and swearing. - Henry Beard & Roy Mckie

Work is for those who don't know how to fish.

Well stocked rivers, lakes and streams,
These are a fisherman's favourite dreams.

When I'm tired and I can't sleep,
I count fishes instead of sheep.

FRIENDSHIP

True friends listen when no one else hears.

Friendship isn't a big thing
It's a million little things.

Friendship grows from pleasures shared.
- Charles Dickens

The only way to have a friend is to be one. - Ralph Waldo Emerson

I cherish you
You're sweet and kind,
A truer friend I'll never find.

Best friends like you
do and say
the nicest things
in the sweetest way

Our friendship is like a cup of tea,
a special blend of you & me

Friendships are
glued together with kindness.

What are Friends For:
To cheer on,
share with,
learn from,
laugh with
& love.

Life is filled with simple joys
and blessings without end
but one of my greatest joys in life
is to count you as my dear friend.

Like fine wine,
friends get better with time

"Stay" is a charming word in a
friend's vocabulary.
- Mary Alcott

Don't let grass grow
on the path of friendship.
- Native American proverb

Funny Bone Ticklers

Macho doesn't prove Mucho

HOME OF THE
Lawn Ranger

Men are just a bunch of animals...
but some do make good pets

Everytime I give my husband an inch
he starts to think he's a ruler!

I'm saving my husband
lot$ of money
I buy EVERYTHING I SEE
ON $ALE

Only
mothers of teenagers
can understand how
animals can eat their young

I love to get stressed
but only when spelled backwards.
(desserts)

I am woman,
I am invincible.....
I am tired.

Money is the root of all evil....
and I need to feel rooted.

Not again.....
too much month
at the end of the money.

Girls just wanna have fund$.

Funny Bone Ticklers

Entering a Positive Thinking Area

Will the answer to this question be "No"?

What good are laurels if you can't rest on them?

Prisoner at a chocolate factory
DON'T send Help.

It's been one of those days
all week!

No brain
No headache

If the tv and the fridge weren't so far apart
we'd never get any exercise.

If you smoke....
don't exhale.

A journey of 1000 steps begins with
trying to find a parking spot.

Panic Button
Press here

You don't have to brush all your teeth....
just the ones you want to keep.

Go ahead
take my advice,
I'm not using it anyway.

I'm so far behind
I thought I was first

Everyone has a Mother-in-Nature.

Nature wears a universal grin

- Henry Fielding

iracles grow where you plant them.

What is a weed?
A plant whose virtues have not yet been discovered.

- Ralph Waldo Emerson

Garden of Love Recipe

- water with kindness
- weed out resentment.
- nurture with compassion

The flowers of all tomorrows
are in the seeds of today.

- Chinese proverb

Nature is the art of God.

The touch of nature makes the whole world kin.

- William Shakespeare

A garden is a friend
you can visit anytime.

Gardening grows the Spirit.

Have a Bloomin Good Day

This garden is grown with love.

Heaven is under our feet
as well as over our heads
- Henry David Thoreau

From the earth we were formed,
to the earth we return....
and in between we garden.

If you truly love nature,
you will find beauty everywhere
- Vincent Van Gogh

I dig the earth.

Flower Power

Like life,
few gardens have only flowers.

One is nearer to God's heart
in a garden,
than anywhere else on earth.
- Dorothy Gurney

We all need to be rooted
in order to blossom.

nd kind spirits amid a Garden
nd thoughts become the roots
nd words grow the flowers
nd kind deeds are surely the fruits.

Earth is crammed with heaven

To golf or not to golf?
What a silly question.

/hen's tee time?

GOLF :
a day spent in a round
of strenuous idleness.
- William Wordsworth

.cret to good golf:
Hit hard, straight
and not too often.

GOLF is the most fun you can have
without taking your clothes off.
- Chi Chi Rodrigueez

I GOLF
therefore I am not here.

'm not over the hill........
just on the back nine.

Golf has created more liars
than income tax
(the IRS or Revenue Canada)

Bye Bye Birdie

A GOLFER'S CHIEF HANDICAP IS HIS HONESTY
- MacLeans

I live with fear every day...
t sometimes she lets me go golfing

Golfer's Prayer
May I live long enough
to shoot my age.

Golf is a good walk spoiled.
- Mark Twain

Mind Your Mummy & Deaddy

TOMB SWEET TOMB

Welcome Every-Batty

Halloween

Boo — Boo — Boo — Boo

Pumpkins come and pumpkins go
But a jack-o-lantern steals the show.

TREAT...OR ELSE

Oops..... Bat Breath

Twick or Tweet

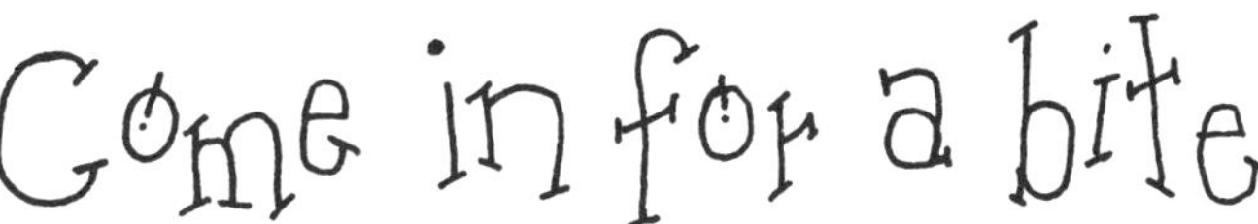

Sounds Fangtastic

Love at 1st bite

The Ghostess With the Mostess!

Ghosts have real spirit!

Have a Hauntingly Happy Howl-ween

Fangs for the memories and nightmares.

Hobbies

Hunters will do anything for a buck.

The smell of fresh sawdust
is sweeter to me,
than any rose could ever be.

When in doubt...
route

Rules 4 Tools
Put'em back or
catch the flack

Workshop Rule
Don't mess with my mess

Sawdust means
Work in Progress

Woodworkers are a cut above the board.

Baseball players are rich in diamonds.

BEWARE:
Computer bytes

I craft, therefore I am.

Quiltn

I needle-lil love.

A quilt is pieces of love
stitched together.

a stitch in
time
saves nine

Born 2 Bingo

Dancers have happy feet!

Happiness is Home brewed

HOME

Home is where we hang our memories

Charity begins at home.

- English proverb
14th century

Home is the warmth of loving hearts.

Bless this home with the music of laughter.

Welcome to the Lake

Heaven seems a little closer in a house by the water

We may not have it all together... but together we have it all

We get along in our R.V. cuz we don't have room to disagree.

Home to laughter, home to rest, Home to those we love the best!

Laughter is sunshine in a house.

A small house can hold as much happiness as a large one.

Our guests make us happy, Some in coming, Some in going.

Welcome to our Zoo!

place for everything
and everything in its place.

- Isabelle Beeton, 1861

Real men Do housework

HOUSEWORK STINKS

Every mother is a working mother.

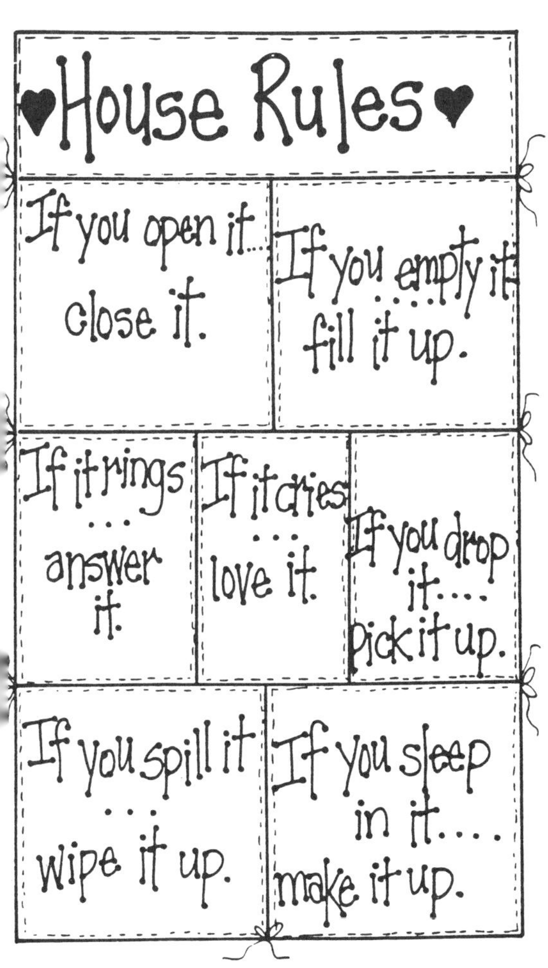

It's the maid's day off...
Don't trip on the dust balls

I only have a kitchen
cuz it came with the house.

Around here "normal"
is just a setting on the dryer.

No....Martha Stewart does not live here.

leaning your house
ile your kids are still growing,
 like shovelling the walk
fore it stops snowing.

- Phyllis Diller

Please excuse the mess
We just really want you to feel at home.

The Queen does not do dishes

Inspiration

Inch by inch
any goal is a cinch.

No goals-
No glory.

Opportunity never comes.....
It's here.

Don't agonize - organise.

People with tact
have less to retract.

Genius is 1% inspiration
99% perspiration.
- Thomas Edison

Don't be-little
Be Big.

An open mind opens doors.

Happiness is an inside job.

Turn a frown upside down.

Happiness
is just a smile away.

Mud thrown
is ground lost.

Carpe Diem
Seize the Day

Laugh often,
Learn much
and love life
with all your heart.

There's no I in team.

Every life is a story.....
make yours a best seller.

An open mind opens doors.

Don't count the days,
Make the days count.

We can't spell success
without "U."

Even Superman tries to fly higher and faster.

All the wonders you seek
are within yourself.

Quitters never win
Winners never quit.

A journey of 1000 miles begins with but a single step.
- Lao Tzu

People with tact
have less to retract.

Do the worst first!

Don't itch for anything
that you're not willing to scratch for.

Spoonfuls of love added to every recipe.

Kitchen Quips

Happiness is lickin' the spoon

Gossip is harder to unspread than butter.

If life seems too tough, don't cook it so long.

God Blesses this Kitchen
(he doesn't clean it)

Fish

to taste right
must swim
3 times...
in water
in butter
in wine

French Proverb

I love hugs,
I love kisses,
But don't forget,
I also love
HELP WITH THE DISHES.

Give us this day our daily bread

Homemade with Love
from my kitchen.

Homemade and Good
4 - U - 2

I never met a cookie I didn't like.

Before my first cup of coffee I'm a bear!

Everything you see, I owe to spaghetti.

- Sophia Loren

Coffee Java
To bean or not to bean?

Money can't buy love......
but it can buy caffé mocchas.

Latte Da ...
Latte Da ...

Things taste better in small houses

- Queen Victoria

Peas be with you

Conserve Water....
Drink wine.

One thing for sure.... there is no sure thing.

n The experience of This sweet Life
- Dante

hen you worry about what the whole world is coming to.... Remember so did Grandpa.

View life by smiles, not by tears and age by great moments, not by years.

If you want to break a habit Drop it!

An eye for an eye only make the whole world go blind.

God is inside each of us.

n not sure if life is passing me by or trying to run me over.

The problem with doing nothing is.... you never know when you are done.

ife has a way of passing you by, passionately if you sing it, boring if you sigh.

Life is the greatest bargain, We get it for nothing.

Another day, Another play.

Love is a hug

LOVE

The ♡ that loves is always young.

- Greek proverb

If you would be loved,
love and be lovable.

- Benjamin Franklin

All works of love
are works of peace.

- Mother Teresa

Love means holding hands
not grudges.

Forget love....
Let's fall in chocolate!

Love conquers all

- Virgil

To love, is to receive a glimpse of heaven.

- Karen Sunde

Miles apart
but always
close in ♥

In the end the love you take
is equal to the love you make.

- John Lennon

The happiest people in the world
are the ones who help spread it!

I made a wish
and you came true.

as far as I can see...
your the best little gift
ever given to me.

Love wasn't put in your heart to stay
Love isn't love until you give it away.

You complete me.

- Jerry MaGuire

Love can't grow
until you give some away.

All you need is love.

- John Lennon

Your love gives a glow to my soul.

Loved you yesterday,
love you still,
always have and always will.

One is very crazy
when in love

- Sigmund Freud

Love is a springtime plant
that perfumes everything with hope.

- Flaubert

Joy is a net of love
by which you can catch souls.

You take ordinary moments
and make them shine.

I'm not over the hill yet, I can't get up it.

Over the hill

Been there,
Done that...
Can't remember

Don't resent growing older,
nany are denied the privilege

It's sad to grow old,
but nice to ripen.

- Bridgette Bardot

I'm a valuable antique
with hair full of silver,
teeth full of gold,
and joints full of lead

I'm too young to be this old!

Baldness – the cure for dandruff

rrow old along with me,
the best is yet to be.

- Robert Browning

It's better gray than nay

Cheap Facelift - SMILE

I shall grow old but never lose lifes zest,
because the roads last turn shall be the best

- Henry Van Dyke

I've become a
iable, Historic Monument.

Age is only a number

Let's play connect the dots
with all our little liver spots

Look 30,
Act 20,
Feel 60
Must be 40

Don't take life so seriously,
it's not permanent.

It takes a long time to grow old

Pablo Picasso

Seasons come and seasons go, captured here the sweetest memories we know

Photo Quips

clic clic clic

Hearts Forever Entwined

Good Moo's from the Herd We've added one udder.

A match made in Heaven

I'm a Miracle!

Fond Memories of Family, Friends & Fun Times

It's not easy being a princess

Presenting Her (His) Royal Highness

cute as a button

We is terrific!

CK: cute kid

123 ABC School Daze ABC 123

Best Buddies

Our Little Angels

Barnyard Buddies

Be humble? Impossible! We're the Grandparents!

Girl Friends Forever

Fun in the Sun

Grandma's Sweethearts

Grandpa's All Stars

Life's a Beach

A gentle word opens an iron gate. - Bulgarian

The day is lost if no one has not laughed. - French

Manana is often the busiest day of the week. - Spanish

Hold a true friend with both your hands. - Nigerian

Good deeds are the best prayer - Serbian

ith keeps the world going. - Hindi

Every day of your life is a page of your history - Arabic

Beauty without virtue is..... a flower without perfume. - French

No sleep..... No dreams. - Korean

Trust in God..... but tie up your camel. - Iranian

In dreams and in love nothing is impossible. - Hungarian

Before you marry keep both eyes open After marriage, shut one. - Jamaican

ife is the greatest bargain, we get it for nothing
- Yiddish

Earth is dearer than gold
- Estonian

A stumble may prevent a fall. - Chinese

Worry often gives a small thing a big shadow. - Swedish

Loose lips sink ships.
- American

The more you know, The less you need.
- Austrailian Aboriginal

Kind words conquer.
- Asian

You make the road by walking on it.
- Nicaraguan

It takes a 1000 voices to tell a single story.
- Native American

Do good and heaven will come down to you.
Hawaiian

New day... New fate
- Bulgarian

Nature is the art of God
- Latin

The best candle is understanding.
- Welsh

If you are lucky enough to be Irish, you are lucky enough.
- Irish fact

Happy Bearday

Teddies

Don't feed us
We're stuffed.

Stuffed with Love

Best Fur-ends
Fur-ever.

A friend by your side
can keep you warmer
than any fur coat.

Friends ... make everything bearable

SHOW ME
THE HONEY

Bear Collector
Orphans Welcome.

FREE BEAR HUGS
anytime...
any bear

Honey Bee Happy

Bear with
me.

I wish I was a teddy bear...

The more worn out you are
The more valuable you become

Only the most
Special Bears
get their fur all
loved off

Aa Bb Cc Dd Ee Ff

Gg Hh Ii Jj Kk Ll Mm Nn Oo Pp Qq

Aa Bb Cc Dd Ee

Ff Gg Hh Ii Jj Kk

Ll Mm Nn Oo Pp Qq

Rr Ss Tt Uu Vv Ww

Xx Yy Zz &

1 2 3 4 5 6

7 8 9 0

Rr Ss Tt Uu Vv Ww x

y z

Aa Bb Cc Dd Ee Ff Gg Hh

Ii Jj Kk Ll Mm Nn Oo Pp

Qq Rr Ss Tt Uu Vv Ww Xx

Yy Zz. 1 2 3 4 5 6 7 8 9 0

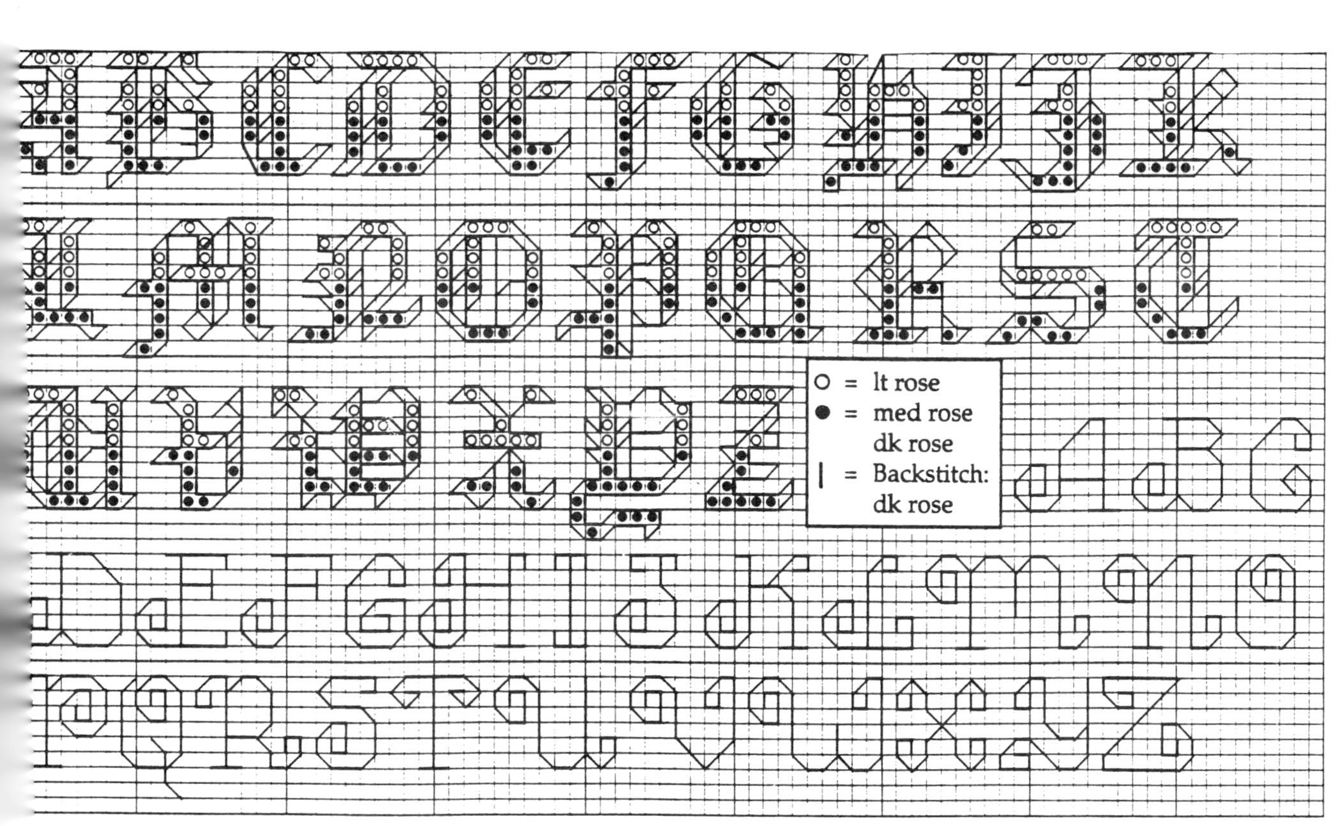